Exploration Into LATIN AMERICA

ANA MARIA MACHADO

new Discovery B·O·O·K·S

Parsippany, New Jersey

First American publication 1995 by New Discovery Books,
an imprint of Silver Burdett Press.
A Simon & Schuster Company,
299 Jefferson Road, Parsippany, NJ 07054.

LIBRARY OF CONGRESS CATALOGING-IN-PUBLICATION DATA

Machado, Ana Maria, 1941-
    Exploration into Latin America / Ana Maria Machado.
    p. cm
    Includes index.
    ISBN 0-02-718084-0 (LSB) 0-382-24970-4 (pbk)
    1. Latin America—History—Juvenile literature. 2. Latin
America—Discovery and exploration—Juvenile literature.
    3. Explorers—Latin America—History—
Juvenile literature. 4. Mayas—Juvenile literature.
    5. Aztecs—Juvenile literature. 6. Incas—Juvenile literature.
    [1. Latin America—Discovery and exploration. 2. Latin America—
History.] I.Title
F1410.M18 1995
918.04—dc20   94–28824

SUMMARY: An explanation of discoveries made in Latin America,
from the beginnings of time up to the 19th century explorers, with
a postscript about the region in modern times.

First published in Great Britain in 1994 by
Belitha Press Limited, London

Printed in Hong Kong

Photographic credits

Ancient Art & Architecture Collection 11, 12 bottom left,
17 bottom left, 22 top left; **Andes Press Agency** 42 top;
Bridgeman Art Library 32 bottom right; Bruce Coleman
Limited cover background; **Sue Cunningham Photographic**
33, 43, bottom, 44 right; **John Curtis** 10; **Dagli Orti** 16 bottom,
18 bottom, 24 top, 39 top; **E.T. Archive** 9 bottom, 19 top right
and middle, 29 top, 36 top; **Mary Evans Picture Library** 2,
26 top, 29 middle, 35 bottom, 40 top right; **Werner Forman
Archive** 13 Dr Kurt Stavenhagen collection, 16 top right
Dallas Museum of Art; Giraudon/Bridgeman Art Library
28 bottom; **Robert Harding Picture Library** 6, 9 top right,
12 bottom right, 17 bottom right, 18 top, 19 top left and
bottom British Museum, 25 National Maritime Museum,
26 bottom, 27 National Martime Museum, 36 bottom British
Museum, 37, 38 top Schloss Tegel, Berlin and bottom; **Hulton
Deutsch** 16 top left, 24 bottom, 28 top, 31, 40 bottom;
Mansell Collection 5, 26/27, 35 top; Impact Photos
(Piers Cavendish) cover foreground; **Andrew Oliver** 22 top
right, 23 bottom, 43 middle, 45, back cover; **Royal
Geographical Society** 3, 7 top and middle right, 8, 9 top left,
39 bottom, 44 left; **Nick Saunders/Barbara Heller** 14 left;
South American Pictures title page, 7 left and bottom right,
12 top, 14 right, 15, 17 top, 21, 22 bottom, 23 top, 29 bottom,
30, 32 bottom left, 40 top left, 41, 42 bottom, 43 top, 44 top.

Editor: Jill Laidlaw
Designer: Andrew Oliver
Picture researcher: Vanessa Kelly
Consultant: Professor John Fisher of the Institute
of Latin American Studies at Liverpool University
Series consultant: Shane Winser, Royal
Geographical Society, London
Map annotations: Hardlines

This page: **T**his
*French engraving of
1855 reveals the Maya
pyramid of Papantla
in Mexico.*

Previous page: **A**n
*Aymara Indian (from
Bolivia) in a traditional
reed boat.*

Contents

An Aymara woman from Lake Titicaca in Bolivia. She is weaving cloth using a traditional loom tied around her back.

NORTH AMERICA

ATLANTIC OCEAN

Valley of Mexico

Florida

Gulf of Mexico

Tula

BAHAMAS

Teotihuacan • Lake Texcoco
Mount • Tenochtitlan
Popocatepetl • Chichen-Itza
• • Monte • Palenque YUCATAN
Alban • Tikal

CUBA

HISPANIOLA

JAMAICA

PUERTO RICO

WEST INDIES

CENTRAL AMERICA

Caribbean Sea

TRINIDAD

Isthmus of Panama

Orinoco River

GUIANA HIGHLANDS

CORDILLERA ORIENTAL

Lake Guatavita

Rio Negro River

Rio Branco River

Mounts of the Amazon River

Amazon River

Mount Chimborazo

Ucayali River

Amazon Basin

AMAZON RAIN FOREST

Madeira River

ANDES MOUNTAINS

Chavín de Huantar

SOUTH AMERICA

BRAZILIAN HIGHLANDS

Machu Picchu
• Sacsahuaman
Cuzco
Paracas • • Lake Titicaca
Nazca • *Altiplano*
• Potosí

PANTANAL

MATO GROSSO

PACIFIC OCEAN

Atacama Desert

GRAN CHACO

Paraguay River

Parana River

PAMPAS

La Plata Estuary

PATAGONIA

The landscapes of Latin America vary a great deal. There are high mountains, rain forests, and beaches of white sand. If you travel inland to the Brazilian northeast, there is a desertlike region where rivers flow for only a few months of the year.

The puma, many species of monkey, the armadillo, the anteater, the llama, the **alpaca**, snakes, crocodiles, lizards, hummingbirds, and parrots are just some of the exotic animals of Latin America.

Cuernos del Paine

Tierra del Fuego

Cape Horn

1 Exploring Latin America

The Story of Latin America

Where Is Latin America?

Latin America is in the western hemisphere and has the Atlantic Ocean on its east side and the Pacific Ocean to the west. America is actually made up of two continents, North and South America, that are linked by Central America. The central and southern parts of this "double" continent are called Latin America.

The Countries of Latin America

The name "Latin America" is quite recent. It first came into use in France around 1860. When we talk about Latin America we think of one North American country (Mexico), the six small **republics** of Central America, three Caribbean countries (Cuba, the Dominican Republic, and Haiti), and all of the Spanish-speaking republics of South America as well as Portuguese-speaking Brazil. Surinam and Guyana are not included in Latin America even though they are in South America.

Exploring This Book

This book is divided into seven chapters. This chapter explains the geography of Latin America. The next chapter is an introduction to some of the first people of Latin America, and the third chapter looks at the great empires of the Mayas, Aztecs, and Incas. The second half of the book (chapters four, five, six, and seven) looks at explorers from the fifteenth to the twentieth centuries.

Amerigo Vespucci

How Did Latin America Get Its Name?

The first Europeans to settle in Latin America were the Spanish, led by Christopher Columbus (1451-1506), an Italian from Genoa. Columbus made other trips to America and brought with him Amerigo Vespucci (1454-1512), an Italian navigator, who wrote about the new land. Amerigo's writings became linked with the area and it was eventually called America, after him.

Latin America also inherits the first part of its name from Italy. The Latins lived in Lazio, the region where Rome was founded. When the Roman Empire became very powerful and conquered almost all of western Europe (first to second centuries A.D.), Latin was spoken everywhere. Later on (fifth century A.D.), Germanic tribes came from the north of Europe and invaded the Roman Empire, but in Portugal, Spain, France, Romania, and Italy, many elements of Roman culture survived. The parts of America that the Spanish and Portuguese explored became known as "Latin America."

An Isolated Land

South America is an isolated continent. It has many animals and plants that are found nowhere else on earth. During **prehistoric** times it was part of one giant land mass, called Pangaea. Over millions of years, this split into two smaller land masses, called Laurasia and Gondwanaland. South America eventually drifted away from Gondwanaland around 100 million years ago.

The Oldest Coast

The eastern coast of Latin America is **geologically** much older than that of the west. Although there are mountains very near the Atlantic Ocean, forming a series of bays and coves full of small islands, they are not as high as the ones on the Pacific shore. From the Andes, great rivers run east into the mighty Amazon River. Another important river, the Paraná-Paraguay, rises in the heart of the continent and reaches the sea at the La Plata **Estuary**. Rivers drop from the mountains in a series of waterfalls and then flow through **fertile** plains to the beginning of the **pampas**.

The Pantanal is a unique region in the middle of the continent, covered with fields and forests that are flooded for half of the year. These fields are the natural habitat for rare species of fish, birds, and reptiles. It is the world's largest wetland.

These are the Eastern Cordillera Mountains of Bolivia. Cordillera means "chain" in Spanish.

The first people to come to North America crossed over from Asia via a massive sheet of ice 10,000 years ago. Some moved south to Latin America.

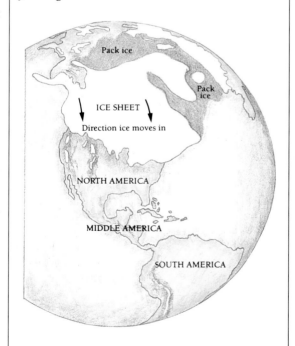

Rain Forests and Mountains

Parts of Latin America are **tropical** and do not have four different seasons like Europe and North America. Along the western coast there are some very high snow-covered mountains that contrast with the almost-constant summer of the rest of the continent. A series of rivers flow east from these mountains to make up some important **fluvial basins**. Among them is the biggest one on earth —the Amazon Basin.

The Amazon River flows from the west to the east, roughly along the line of the **equator**, to form a great mass of water at the hottest point on the planet. A large part of this water **evaporates** and then falls as rain. This combination of rain and hot weather helped to form the Amazonian rain forest, which is full of exotic animals and plants.

This is the Ucayali River winding through the Peruvian rain forest. The Ucayali flows into the Amazon, the world's second longest river.

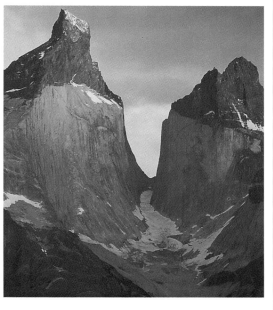

Latin America's landscape varies greatly. This is the dramatic Cuernos del Paine Mountain in Chile. Cuernos means "horn" in Spanish.

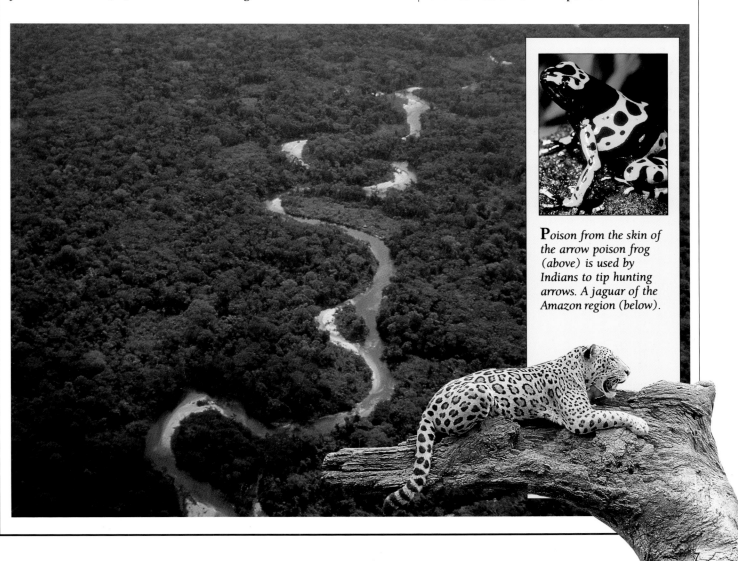

Poison from the skin of the arrow poison frog (above) is used by Indians to tip hunting arrows. A jaguar of the Amazon region (below).

2 The Birth of a Culture

Primitive Peoples

The beginnings of human agriculture in Latin America have been found in Ecuador dating from 6600 B.C. and in Mexico from 5000 B.C. onward. By c. 2000 B.C. many thousands of farming villages existed all over Latin America. The people in these settlements hunted rabbits and deer and relied on plants for shelter, clothes, furniture, food, weapons, and containers. Potatoes were the main ingredient of any diet, and the first people of the Andes managed to breed different types of potatoes to thrive in different types of soil. Eventually, these farmers found a way of "freeze-drying" food. The potatoes were left outside in the cold all night and then in the sun all day. Every day, the family would walk over the potatoes to squeeze the water out of them. After about a week the potatoes became very light chunks of food that could be stored for up to six years. These dried potatoes were soaked in water before they were eaten.

Modern-day Callaway Indians (from Amarete) harvest potatoes in much the same way as their ancestors did 4,000 years ago.

Some of the places where early human remains have been found in Latin America

8

Ancient Latin American people grazed llamas just like these on the Ulla Ulla plateau in Bolivia.

Wandering Peoples

Many of the first people of Latin America were nomadic —this means that they traveled in small groups from one place to another living on fruit, animals, and fish. Some tribes settled, built villages, and grew maize (a type of corn), **manioc**, and other roots. People made flour and bread from what they harvested, but they did not have cattle or other animals to help them to farm the land. The only domestic animals they had were the llama, the alpaca, the guinea pig, and a kind of tame dog that could not bark.

The First Civilizations

Civilizations first developed in the central Andes (Peru and Bolivia), Mexico, and northern Central America. Hunters and fishermen settled in villages and began farming the land and sea from 2000 to 1400 B.C. Because the land and sea were very fertile and the inhabitants good farmers and fishermen, the populations of these communities grew very rapidly. Food was easily produced, so time became available to develop architecture, religion, cities, armies, pottery, and art. The early peoples of Latin America also found time to explore their own land extensively, considering all travel was on foot.

What Grows in Latin America?

Many Latin American plants are known worldwide. Corn, tomatoes, potatoes, tobacco, cocoa beans (used for making chocolate and cosmetics), and fruits like pineapples and avocados all came from Latin America. Other **native** plants include manioc, many kinds of **yams** and sweet potatoes, medicinal herbs, and a large variety of woods, used both for construction and as sources of dyes for **textile** manufacturers.

A *seventeenth-century painting of an Aztec using a digging stick to plant corn (above). An Inca serving dish and maize cobs (below). Maize was made into porridge and tortillas (pancakes) and served with beans.*

A map showing the territories of some early northern Andean, Colombian, and Ecuadorean cultures. Discoveries of some of the earliest remains of pottery, dating from 4000 to 3000 B.C. have been made in modern-day Colombia and Ecuador. The northern Andean cultures are famous for the objects they made out of gold. Other Andean people, such as the Paracas, specialized in depicting complicated stories in cloth.

This is an artist's reconstruction of the Nazca people making their great drawings in the desert.

Early Andean Cultures

The main temple of Chavín de Huantar. The Spanish soldiers who came here in the sixteenth century thought that the city had been built by giants.

Influential Cultures

Of all the early cultures of Latin America, one of the most fascinating is known as the Chavín. The Chavín were only discovered and explored in 1919 by the Peruvian **archaeologist** Julio Tello. We don't know much about the Chavín except that they built a religious center in a small valley near the village of Chavín de Huantar in Peru. This settlement consists of beautiful temples dating from the height of their power (850-200 B.C.). Chavín culture mastered complicated farming and building techniques and made textiles, pottery, and objects out of gold. This culture had a great influence on neighboring societies.

This fragment of Paracas cloth (300-100 B.C.) shows a cat god with a long tongue that ends in a human head.

Decorating the Desert

The Paracas (600-200 B.C.), also from Peru, were influenced by the Chavín. The Paracas spoke Quechua, which is the second official language of modern-day Peru. From the human remains that have been found we know that these people knew how to perform complicated skull operations. They also made intricate embroideries and beautiful pottery. The Paracas decorated the desert with huge images, drawn in the soil, that can still be seen today.

The Nazca

Other "desert artists" include the Nazca (100-1000 A.D.) of Peru, who were also influenced by the Chavín. The Nazca made huge drawings on the ground by removing the dark surface gravel of the earth to reveal the light-colored rock underneath. These pictures of birds and animals can be seen only from the air and we still do not understand their meaning.

The Moche

The culture of the Moche people, in the Moche Valley, thrived for 600 years from the start of Christianity. The Moche built the Pyramid of the Sun out of mud and straw (called adobe) in the middle of their valley over hundreds of years. This huge pyramid was the largest structure of its kind in Latin America.

The Moche grew enough peppers, peanuts, potatoes, and maize on their desert coastline to feed themselves and trade with other peoples inland. Moche artists were very skilled in making pottery, weaving, and gold- and silversmithing.

A *pre-Columbian gold mask from Ecuador of a woman with jade eyes*

The Gold Artists

One of the most advanced people were the Muiscas of what is now Colombia. The Muiscas lived between the Maya people to the north and the Quechua-speakers to the south. The Muiscas were part of the Chibcha-speaking peoples who lived across Central and South America.

The Muiscas built cities out of clay, wood, and palms. Their chief, or Bogotá, was adored as if he were a god. Like other Chibcha people in Colombia, such as the **Tairona**, the **Sinu**, the **Quimbaya**, and the **Tolima**, they made gold into an amazing variety of beautiful objects, often encrusted with emeralds.

The treasures of the last Bogotá caused his death and the end of the Chibcha kingdom. In 1537 the Spanish came looking for gold (see pages 24-33) and the Muiscas were defeated in spite of fierce resistance.

A *gold chest decoration made by the Tolima people of Colombia*

From the Sea to the Land

The Andean culture of the Chorrera (1200-300 B.C.) in Ecuador also had widespread influence. These people abandoned their traditional seafaring way of life and traveled inland to grow maize and manioc. Their society became very prosperous and they developed new techniques for producing pottery.

People Start to Mix

Many Andean societies (especially those in what is now Peru, Ecuador, Bolivia, and Colombia) began to mix and explore each others' cultures because of the trade routes between them. This time, from the sixth to the end of the fifteenth centuries, is known as the Integration Period.

The City of Chan Chan

The Chimú people built the great city of Chan Chan on one side of the Moche Valley at the edge of the sea. The Chimú ruled the Lambayeque Valley from about 1350 A.D. until they were absorbed into the Inca Empire (see pages 21-23) around 1470. Chan Chan consists of about ten large walled "mini-cities" that cover about two square miles. No one really knows how each city functioned but modern-day archaeologists think that when a Chimú ruler died, he was sealed up in his city, rather like a huge grave. Another city was then built for the next king.

A *giant stone figure from highland Bolivia dating from 600 A.D.*

This *is a ceramic cup bearing the portrait of a ruler of the Moche people of northern Peru (powerful from the first to the seventh centuries).*

Early Mexican Cultures

In Mexico and Central America people were not as isolated as in the Andes. Different communities had many things in common, such as large cities, pyramids, a great variety of gods, human sacrifice, a 365-day calendar, and hieroglyphs (a type of writing). The peoples of Mexico and Central America also farmed the same type of foods such as maize, beans, chili, and peppers. Instead of many powerful communities existing separately at the same time, as in the Andes, different groups of people rose to power and dominated the others during different stages of history. All the cultures of Mexico and Central America influenced each other at one time or another.

Olmecs and Zapotecs

The Olmecs (1200-400 B.C.) came from the shores of the Gulf of Mexico and gradually moved into the highlands. The Olmecs could feed a large population because their farming land was rich and was flooded regularly by surrounding rivers. Their culture produced religious monuments, cave paintings, and beautiful sculptures that had a lasting effect on later civilizations.

When the Olmec culture declined, the Zapotecs (800-500 B.C.) were one of the largest groups left in the highlands. Their pottery and sculpture were remarkable and they used advanced methods of **irrigation** for farming.

Places where early Mexican cultures thrived are shown on this map.

This Olmec figure of a baby crying is made out of terra-cotta.

This Olmec sculpture of a ruler from San Lorenzo in Mexico is about 10 feet tall.

The City of Teotihuacán

Among all the early Mexican peoples, none were more powerful than those who built the city of Teotihuacán in the Valley of Mexico. This civilization dates from the beginning of Christianity to 600 and had a great influence over the rest of Mexico.

Teotihuacán was probably the capital of a mighty empire, but no written documents have been found relating to it and we know very little about the people who built it. We do know that these people explored the lands to the south and controlled the Maya area (see map on page 15) and that they were successful traders who employed thousands of artists to produce tools and pottery for export to neighboring areas.

The Zapotecs ruled from the city of Monte Albán (top picture). Monte Albán is on top of a hill and consists of a huge pyramid surrounded by smaller temples on raised platforms.

Worshiping the Sun and the Moon

Teotihuacán was much larger than any city in Europe of the same period. The center of the city covered more than 7 square miles and was built in a grid pattern. It is thought that the city was inhabited by 125,000-250,000 people in more than 5,000 buildings including at least 2,500 private houses. Teotihuacán had wide streets, temples, tunnels, and priests' houses. The two main buildings were pyramids dedicated to the sun and the moon. The pyramids were covered in white plaster and then decorated with brightly colored mythological scenes. Even after the city's power declined it was of great importance to the Aztecs (see pages 18-20), who made **pilgrimages** to it.

This fierce pottery head was found buried with its owner in the city of Teotihuacán.

A plan of the center of the city of Teotihuacán

3 The Great Empires

The Mayas

As Great As the Romans

Many Maya sites were discovered by the American John Lloyd Stephens (1805-1852), and the Englishman Frederick Catherwood (1799-1854), on their difficult expeditions through Mexico and Central America from 1839 to 1840 and 1841 to 1842. Catherwood drew many of the cities and **artifacts** that he and Stephens found. When the pair's books were published they revealed the huge temples, palaces, weapons, and jewels of the Maya civilization. The Mayas were powerful when the Roman Empire ruled Europe (18 centuries ago). The Maya Empire was powerful from c. 300 to 900 A.D., but by the time the Europeans arrived in Latin America in 1492, the Maya Empire had already collapsed because of **civil wars** and invasions by other native groups. The Mayas were succeeded by the Toltecs (see box on page 17) and then the Aztecs (see pages 18-20), who fought the Spaniards in Mexico at the time of the European conquest in the sixteenth century.

The main cities of the Maya's civilization are shown on the map above. The small boxed map shows the area of Latin America where the Mayas lived.

The Maya temples of Tikal push out of the rain forest of Guatemala. Fifty thousand people lived in houses built on mounds in the 6 square miles around Tikal.

Counting and Writing

Hieroglyphs engraved on monuments prove that the Mayas had an alphabet. We also know that the Mayas had a very accurate system of mathematics that was used to work out complex measurements and **equations**. The Maya calendar was more exact than the European one of the same time, with the year divided into 18 months, each 20 days long. At the end of the year there were five days for celebrations and every four years there was an extra day that made the year a leap year.

A colored engraving by Catherwood of the temple of Tulum, from Incidents of Travel in Central America, Chiapas and Yucatán *by Stephens and Catherwood*

This is a drawing of a ball player (above), from a Maya vase (c.500-900 A.D.). The ball was made of solid rubber and was passed between two opposing teams, who were not allowed to touch it with their hands.

This map shows where the Toltecs originally came from in Central America.

The Maya Temple of the Sun and Palace of Palenque in modern-day Mexico.

Cities and Fields

The wealth of the Maya civilization was based on farming, especially maize. The fertile fields made the empire rich and a large population could be fed. The people used their wealth to build cities and create works of art. Some of the cities were surrounded by huge stone walls. Houses were arranged around a large central space where temples and palaces were built. Each Maya city was a state in itself with its own government and laws.

The Toltecs and Chichimecs

From 900 A.D. to the time of the Spanish conquest (see pages 24-33) we have much more information about the people of Latin America because archaeologists have learned to read the records these people left behind. We know that the Toltecs (900-1200 A.D.) came from the north and were hunters and warriors who introduced the bow and arrow to the Maya region. The Toltecs mixed with the Chichimec people and together they founded the city of Tula.

These military statues are in the Toltec capital city of Tula.

The Plumed Serpent

Maize was so important to the Mayas that it was worshiped like a god. Maize had different names depending on whether it was young, sweet, or ripe. A snake with feathers, the Plumed Serpent, represented the god that created everything, including maize. The Mayas believed that this serpent had taught people peace. On huge Maya temples and palaces every inch of the stone was decorated in honor of the gods, and works of art were created as offerings to the gods.

A Maya statue of a man with the head of a jaguar (600-900 A.D.).

Around 1200 the Mayas were defeated by the Toltecs from the north. Maya architecture, art, and religion were absorbed by the Toltecs and later passed on to the Aztecs.

The Aztecs

Worshiping with Blood

In 1345, the Aztec tribe from the north traveled to the center of Mexico. They founded Tenochtitlán, a large city on a lake, and ruled over the other tribes in the area. The Aztecs were feared and hated warriors who charged high taxes that made them very rich. The Aztecs believed that the gods had died in order to create the sun and that men should repay the gods with the "sacred water" of human blood.

This mural by Diego Rivera (1886-1957) depicts his impression of the building of Tenochtitlán.

This map shows the extent of the Aztec Empire up until 1519. Tlaxcallan and Teotitlán were independent states within the Aztec Empire.

This illustration from the History of the Indies of New Spain by Diego Duran of 1581 shows Aztecs sacrificing a human being in a religious ceremony.

This Aztec calendar stone would have been looked after by the priests dedicated to the worship of the sun. The calendar was used for recording religious festivals.

Learning from the Toltecs

In 1440, Emperor Montezuma I improved Tenochtitlán by building **aqueducts** and converting part of the lake into farming land. The wealth and peace of the Aztec Empire attracted Toltec workers and merchants who taught the Aztecs how to make objects out of feathers and gold. The Toltecs also taught the Aztecs how to observe and interpret the stars and how to use a calendar.

The Hero Who Became a God

The Plumed Serpent god of the Mayas and Toltecs was renamed Quetzalcoatl by the Aztecs. In Aztec legend, Quetzal was a hero who was changed into a beautiful bird with long tail feathers who looked like a serpent. The Aztecs believed that this god-hero had been defeated by an evil god and had disappeared with a small group of warriors into the eastern sea. Legend foretold that he would return, at the head of white-skinned, bearded men, to defeat his enemies.

The god Quetzalcoatl in an Aztec drawing of the sixteenth century

Building Islands

According to legend, the Aztecs went in search of a place that had been promised to them by the gods. They had been told to find an eagle sitting on a cactus, holding a snake in its beak (see illustration above). They found the eagle on a rock on an island in the middle of Lake Texcoco and settled there. The Mexican national flag displays this symbol today. Texcoco was one of five connected lakes in a valley 6,000 feet above sea level surrounded by volcanoes. Because the island was small, the Aztecs used mud from the bottom of the lake to add more land around the island's edge, but only the land in the center could support stone buildings. The Aztecs built new islands by piling mud on to beds of straw inside wooden fences fixed by stones. As the city grew, channels of water served as streets. The city-dwellers fished in the channels and the lake and grew vegetables on the fertile land of the new islands. Parts of these floating gardens survive today in Mexico City, at Xochimilco.

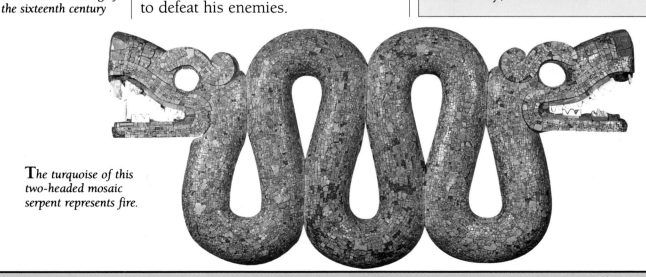

The turquoise of this two-headed mosaic serpent represents fire.

19

Aztec Life

It is thought that the Aztec Empire consisted of more than ten million people at its height in the early sixteenth century. Such a large empire needed powerful leadership and warriors became very important in Aztec society. Merchants traveled through the empire trading goods and also acting as spies. A great many documents were written secretly by a special group of priests, rather like a modern-day secret service. The Aztecs wrote these documents in hieroglyphs on paper made out of tree bark. Writing was an important aspect of Aztec life and the Aztecs wrote lists of taxes, legal documents, religious texts, and their own history books.

Trading was a major part of daily life in the Aztec capital of Tenochtitlán. The peoples of the Aztec Empire brought their goods to Tenochtitlán to trade with its 100,000 inhabitants.

The Aztecs exchanged goods and used cocoa seeds as money because they were easy to carry. More than 60,000 Aztecs went shopping in the capital every day. Their markets were well organized but crowded. They could buy everything from food to slaves, pottery, textiles, and gold. These markets amazed the Spanish soldiers who came to Mexico at the beginning of the sixteenth century. They declared that they had never seen anything to equal them in Europe.

Sacsayhuaman is on the outskirts of the modern city of Cuzco and was the scene of many battles.

The Incas

In ancient times (1500 B.C.–1200 A.D.), there were two main centers of civilization in the Andean region—Nazca, on the Pacific shore, and Tiahuanaco, near Lake Titicaca. But around 1100 A.D., Quechua-speaking Incas came from the south (Lake Titicaca) to the Andes and founded the city of Cuzco. The Incas eventually started to explore and conquer new lands and finally established the most organized empire of Latin America, which was powerful until c.1530. The Incas built large cities and ruled over a vast territory—the equivalent of modern-day Peru, Ecuador, west Bolivia, north Chile, and northwest Argentina.

*The colonial city of Cuzco was built on Inca remains. The **Jesuit** church can be seen in the center.*

A map of the Inca Empire from the time of its first ruler, Manco Capac, who ruled from about 1230, to its final ruler, Huayna Capac, who ruled from 1493 to 1525

A seventeenth-century illustration of the Inca in charge of the quipu

Writing with Knots

The Incas used a system of strings and knots called *quipu* instead of an alphabet. Several strings hung from a main woolen string and each one was knotted. Each knot, or series of knots, represented a certain event or a quantity. These knots look complicated to us but the system worked very well for the Incas.

A seventeenth-century drawing of the founder of Cuzco, Manco Capac, the first Inca

The ruins of the great Inca site of Machu Picchu (below and illustration) were only discovered in 1911. Machu Picchu is only 42 miles from the main center of Cuzco, but it is remote and situated on a thin mountain ridge 2,000 feet above the Urubamba River.

The Child of the Sun

The name "Inca" was originally given to the emperor, who was believed to be the child of the sun. Because the sun was the most powerful Inca god, the emperor (Inca) was a very powerful person. The emblems of the Inca's power were heavy gold discs that hung from his ears and the ears of his family. Family connections were very important in Inca society and each family group formed a clan. Each clan had a leader, but all the clans were controlled by the Inca. The Inca's officials traveled all over the empire to watch over the clans and keep him informed. The Incas built a network of roads that covered the entire empire and yet they didn't have any horses, wheels, or carts. All travel across land was on foot. *Tambos* were small buildings dotted along roads at regular intervals. There were probably about a thousand tambos throughout the empire. A messenger ran from one tambo to the next, where another messenger took over—this was how news was conveyed and laws were issued.

Twenty-five thousand miles of roads (like the one below) were built by the Incas.

The stones are so tightly fitted together in these original Inca walls in Cuzco that it is impossible to slip a sheet of paper between the cracks.

Farmers and Artists

Everybody had to work in Inca society, but no one was paid for the jobs they did. Children helped to protect the crops by chasing birds away. People built stone terraces on the mountain slopes in order to grow food. Aqueducts and channels carried water to the fields, which were fertilized with the droppings of seabirds. Small animals and food were offered to the sun during religious festivals to please the gods and safeguard the harvest. Huge barns were used to store maize and potatoes, which were divided among the ordinary people, the courtiers, and the priests.

Artists were held in such respect that instead of paying taxes, they gave their work to the people. Skills such as weaving, bronze casting, potting, and goldworking were at a very advanced level.

23

4 The Europeans Arrive

Exploration Fever

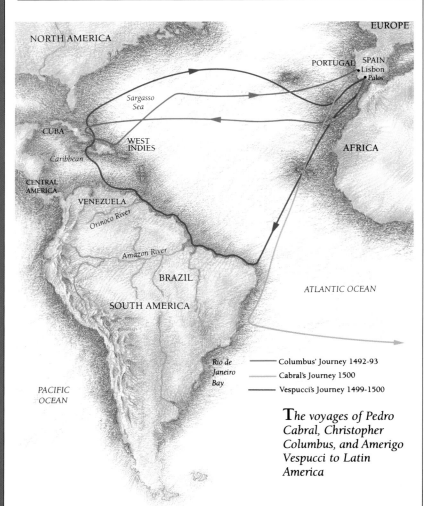

The voyages of Pedro Cabral, Christopher Columbus, and Amerigo Vespucci to Latin America

——	Columbus' Journey 1492-93
——	Cabral's Journey 1500
——	Vespucci's Journey 1499-1500

At the end of the fifteenth century, the lives of the people of Latin America changed forever: the Europeans were about to sail west. They soon arrived, thrust their flags into the ground, and took possession of America.

Christopher Columbus

Christopher Columbus arrived in 1492 sailing under the Spanish flag. His landing almost caused war between Spain and Portugal because both countries claimed rights to "the Indies," as they called this new continent. The Pope intervened and settled the dispute with the Treaty of Tordesillas (1494), which drew a line across the continent from north to south. Lands east of the line belonged to Portugal and lands found to the west belonged to Spain.

A portrait of Christopher Columbus

Exploring for Trade

When Columbus landed in America in 1492, he was looking for a new way to get to the East by sea from Europe. During the Middle Ages (c. 600-1600), all trade between these two areas had been overland in long **caravans** across Asia to Constantinople. But Constantinople had been taken over by the **Turks**, and Europeans were no longer welcome there. European merchants needed new trading routes. The Portuguese explored the African coast in search of a passage to the Indian Ocean. Columbus was convinced that the earth was not flat, which was what most people believed at the time, but was round. He thought that if he sailed to the west, he would finally reach the East. Columbus had no idea that there was an entire continent in between.

This late sixteenth-century drawing shows Columbus being welcomed by natives of the Americas.

A *Dutch painting of Portuguese fighting ships (called carracks) c.1530. It was about this time that the Portuguese explored the coast of Brazil.*

Animals and Gods

At first, the Europeans thought that the people of Latin America were ruled by the great and famous Japanese and Chinese emperors. They also thought that the new lands were as wealthy as the Venetian trader Marco Polo (1254-1324) had written in his famous *Travels of Marco Polo*. Columbus wrote in his diary that he thought he had arrived at "paradise" because the people and the land were so beautiful. But the Europeans soon decided that Indians did not have souls and treated them like animals.

Many Aztec myths were about splendid gods who would come to earth one day (see page 19). When the Spaniards arrived from the east, on horseback and in shining armor, the Indians were overjoyed. They welcomed the Spaniards with open arms as if they were gods (see page 28).

A Race to Get Rich

Columbus made four voyages to America before he finally explored the mainland of Central America in 1502. Meanwhile, the Portuguese had sailed to India for the first time by going around southern Africa. Spain and Portugal were both determined to expand their empires and the two nations were trying to get as rich as possible as quickly as possible—finding new trading routes and lands became important to their success.

New Maps

Each Spanish expedition explored more land, and bit by bit maps were drawn of the unknown continent. At first, only the coastline was known to these new explorers. Some of the men who had accompanied Columbus on his voyages made their own expeditions to northern Latin America. At Maracaibo, they found lake villages and called the region Venezuela, which means "small Venice" in Spanish (after the Italian city). Other men traded pearls and wood with the Indians. In 1499, Vicente Yáñez Pinzón (1460-1524), who had accompanied Columbus on his 1492 voyage, crossed the equator, found the mouth of the Amazon River, and arrived in northeast Brazil.

The Portuguese were also exploring, and after Pedro Cabral (1460-1526) arrived at Brazil in 1500, they explored the south of Latin America. Two years later they reached Rio de Janeiro Bay. Portuguese ships sailed home loaded with the precious red wood of the land, which was called Brazil—the name finally given to the country by Europeans.

In Search of Another Sea

By the beginning of the sixteenth century it was obvious that this new continent was not Asia as the explorers had first thought. The land was too big to be an island and so the search for a route to the Indies went on. Some explorers ventured inland and the Spaniard Vasco Núñez de Balboa (1475-1519) became the first European to see the Pacific Ocean when he crossed the Isthmus of Panama in 1513. But this was not a suitable trading route for ships and so the search for a **passage** to the Pacific Ocean continued. People explored the Amazon River but were disappointed to find that it was not a route to the sea. Farther south, the La Plata Estuary provided no access to the Pacific. Finally, in 1519, the Portuguese voyager Ferdinand Magellan (1480-1521) began his journey of discovery west in one of the most difficult voyages ever made (see box right).

Dividing Up Latin America

In 1534 Charles I of Spain and John III of Portugal decided to **colonize** Latin America. The kings drew straight lines on the map at right angles to the equator. On the Spanish side (west), four huge sections—Nueva Castilla, Nueva Toledo, Nueva Andalucia, and Nueva Leon— were given to captains to govern. East of the line originally agreed to in 1494 in the Spanish town of Tordesillas, the coast of Brazil and the surrounding area was divided into 15 "captainships" (capitanias) and was given to Portuguese noblemen and businessmen who could afford to colonize them.

Around the World

Magellan and his crew lived with the Indians of southern Argentina for a while during their freezing winter. The Indians wore thick fur wound around their feet and the sailors called them *Patagones*, which means "big feet." Magellan explored the small rivers, islands, and dangerous rocks of the coast. He was helped by the Onas Indians, who lit bonfires along the shore to guide the explorer's ships. Because of these bonfires, Magellan called the place Fire Land, or Tierra del Fuego.

Once the passage had finally been discovered, Magellan started a two-month crossing of the Pacific Ocean. Under the blazing sun water became undrinkable, food went rotten, and the men were forced to eat rats, sawdust, and leather. When they arrived at the islands which are now known as the Philippines, in 1521, Magellan was killed in an attack by the natives. Under the leadership of his lieutenant, Juan Sebastián de Elcano (1476-1526), his crew carried on and finally arrived back in Spain later in 1521. After three years of traveling, having survived fire, ice, storms, and mutiny, they arrived home. They were the first people to sail around the world.

A portrait of Ferdinand Magellan

A sixteenth-century engraving of Vasco Núñez de Balboa

This late sixteenth-century engraving shows a popular European view of the cruelty of the Spanish conquest of Peru (see page 29).

The journeys of
Ferdinand Magellan,
Sir Francis Drake,
Vasco Núñez de Balboa,
and Vicente Yáñez Pinzón
to Latin America

Pinzón's Journey 1499–1500
Drake's Journey 1577–80
Magellan's Journey 1519–21
Balboa's Journey 1513

God and Gold

In their search for new trading routes by sea, the conquerors
had discovered new lands. They found that most of the
inhabitants were friendly and worshiped many gods. The
new visitors also came with Roman Catholic priests who
tried to convert the Indians to Christianity. But many
priests, soldiers, and sailors came to Latin America in search
of gold, silver, pearls, gems, and slaves and they were
prepared to kill entire communities to get them.

A portrait of Sir Francis Drake

Drake the Pirate!

Some years after Magellan's voyage,
Elizabeth I of England sent Sir Francis
Drake (1545-1596) on a voyage around
the world. Drake had already attacked
Spanish ships and lands in the
Caribbean. After reaching the Pacific
Ocean, Drake sailed along the coast so
that he could raid Spanish colonies in
Chile and Peru. Nobody expected his
surprise attacks and he captured a great
deal of gold.

27

A *nineteenth-century European drawing of Spanish monks destroying Mexican religious statues.*

Exploring to Conquer

The Conquest of Mexico

Mexico was conquered from 1519 to 1521 by the Spaniard Hernán Cortés (1485-1547), who arrived with guns, horses, and fierce dogs. When he landed with his men, Cortés ordered his ships to be dismantled so that they could not return home. The Aztec emperor, Montezuma, sent Cortés presents – including a golden image of the sun and a silver moon as big as a cartwheel. These offerings made Cortés greedier and more anxious to get to the capital of Tenochtitlán. Cortés made alliances with Montezuma's enemies, destroyed Aztec temples and cities, and erected crosses on the ruins.

Quetzalcoatl was the Aztec god of crossroads, and when the Aztecs saw the Spaniard's Christian crosses, they were convinced that the white, bearded men of ancient legend had arrived from the east as gods (see page 19). At the capital, Montezuma welcomed Cortés as if he were the god Quetzalcoatl. When the Spaniards opened fire on a religious procession, the Indians realized their mistake and started fighting. The Spaniards besieged the city for months until the Aztecs were finally defeated.

A *portrait of Hernán Cortés by the Master of Saldana (left)*

The journeys of Hernán Cortés and Francisco Pizarro through Latin America

Gulf of Mexico

Cortés' Journey 1518-19

Havana
CUBA

Tenochtitlán
Cholula
Acapulco
Veracruz

NEW SPAIN

PACIFIC OCEAN

Panama

Quito

Tumbes

Pizarro's Journey 1531-33

Trujillo

PERU

Lima

ANDES MOUNTAINS

Cuzco

A *European painting of the last battle for Mexico. Cortés is dressed in armor and is waving his sword from the back of his horse in the foreground.*

The Conquest of Peru

The Inca emperor Huayna Capac died shortly before the Spaniards captured Peru. His death was followed by a civil war between his two sons, Huascar (who controlled southern Peru) and Atahualpa (who controlled Ecuador). The Spaniard Francisco Pizarro (1470-1541) arrived in Peru in 1532 to find the country already devastated by civil war. Pizarro had been planning his expedition for a long time because he had heard of the fabulous wealth of the Incas. He brought with him 180 armed men, 37 horses, and some interpreters. Pizarro invited Atahualpa to a meeting but when he arrived, Pizarro's men killed Atahualpa's soldiers and arrested him.

Buying Freedom

In order to buy his freedom, Atahualpa offered the ransom of a small room filled once with gold and twice with silver. It took the Incas many months to collect this treasure from all the corners of their empire. Even 700 gold plaques from the Temple of the Sun in Cuzco were included. One fifth of the treasure was intended as an offering to the king of Spain and each soldier received a fortune. But Atahualpa did not buy his freedom because Pizarro had him strangled. After Atahualpa's death it was easy for Pizarro to conquer the rest of Peru by the end of 1533.

A *popular eighteenth-century engraving of Francisco Pizarro*

The execution of Atahualpa in 1532 as depicted in 1615 by the artist Guaman Poma de Ayala

Legendary Treasures

This pre-Columbian gold mask has eyes of platinum that are hung from tiny wires. It was treasure like this that the conquistadors were in search of.

Aguirre de Lope (c.1510-1561) joined an expedition of 300 men in Peru to find the treasures of El Dorado in 1560. The party left Lima, crossed the Andes, and followed the Huallaga and Marañon rivers. When they reached the Amazon, Aguirre led a mutiny and then took his men down the Amazon raiding villages as he went. Aguirre was captured and executed in 1561.

The fabulous treasures the conquerors took from the Aztecs and the Incas were nothing compared with the legend of El Dorado. After the civilizations that really existed were conquered, the search for mythical golden cities and treasures began in earnest.

The Search for El Dorado

The most enduring Latin American legend was that of El Dorado—the Gold Man. This story probably originated from a Muisca religious ritual. The Muisca Indians (see box on page 12) were part of the Chibcha tribe who lived in the highlands of Colombia near an almost perfectly round lake. Every year the Indians gave a ceremony to thank the golden god that they believed lived at the bottom of the lake. During the ceremony their chief was anointed with a sticky oil and then sprayed with gold dust until he became a glittering, living statue. At the head of a procession, he went to the lake and paddled a raft to the middle of the

The lake of Guatavita, Colombia, where Chibcha chiefs inspired the legend of El Dorado

water; then he dived in and washed away the gold. On the shore, his people threw emeralds and gold objects into the water as offerings to their god.

Another story told of a kingdom in the rain forest where everybody and everything (except food) was covered with gold that was washed off every day. This story became a part of the El Dorado legend. Many greedy people looked for El Dorado, leaving destruction in their trail. The Spanish king gave Venezuela to the Germans who occupied the land and terrorized the natives in their search for gold. They took 220 pounds of gold but did not find El Dorado.

Some of the rivers European explorers traveled in their search for El Dorado

The Search Continues

The Englishman Sir Walter Raleigh (c.1552-1618) traveled up the Orinoco River with five small boats in 1595 in search of El Dorado. Each boat carried 100 men who had to row against the current. When Raleigh's boats finally came out of the delta, they went on to join the main flow of the Orinoco. Raleigh was amazed at the beauty of the landscape and declared, "we passed the most beautiful country that ever mine eyes beheld."

Raleigh stopped near the village of Morequito at the mouth of the Caroní River and met the head of the village, a man called Topiawari. Topiawari was supposed to be 110 years old and yet he walked many miles through the forest to bring Raleigh presents of food. Raleigh and his men were unable to get up the Caroní River and so they returned to England, taking with them disappointed hopes and more stories of El Dorado.

Pirates!

The French, the English, and the Dutch did not want to accept the division of Latin America as decided by the Treaty of Tordesillas (see pages 24 and 26). These nations wanted a share of the treasures found in the new land. Pirates attacked Spanish and Portuguese ships that returned to Europe loaded with Latin American gold and silver. More European expeditions were organized. France established two colonies in Brazil, and the Dutch ruled the cities and sugar-cane plantations of the Brazilian northeast for 25 years. But these colonists eventually fled from the Portuguese, who decided to protect their interests.

An early seventeenth-century picture of Raleigh taking the Spanish governor of St. Joseph (Trinidad) prisoner in 1595

5 Exploring New Countries

A Silver Mountain

A *seventeenth-century engraving of the local population mining silver from Potosí*

Near the village of Potosí in Bolivia, in 1545, an Indian discovered a mountain that glittered with pure silver. In less than 30 years, Potosí had as many inhabitants as contemporary London. One century later, during a religious celebration, the stones that paved the streets of Potosí were replaced by silver bars—they say that even the horseshoes of Potosí were made of silver. Potosí became a wealthy city where many artists worked for churches, rich households, and palaces. There was so much silver at Potosí that what was transported to Spain in one and a half centuries was equal to three times the existing European stocks of silver at the time.

Modern-day Potosí and the colonial town that grew up around the mountain

A Single Ruler

In 1578, King Sebastian of Portugal disappeared during a battle against the Moors, leaving no heir. The Portuguese crown went to Philip II of Spain in 1580 and the two kingdoms remained united for 60 years. During this time nobody worried about the Tordesillas line (see pages 24, 26, and 31). The Portuguese and their Brazilian-born descendants, the Bandeirantes (also known as the "pathfinders"), seized this opportunity to extend their territory and explore deep into the continent.

At first, the Bandeirantes explored inland to find Indian slaves to work the sugar plantations. But Jesuit priests who had built missions in Paraguay defended the Indians. European slave ships transported African slaves to work the fields of northern Brazil, so the emphasis of the Bandeirante expeditions changed. They began to look for precious metals and gems instead of slaves.

A *portrait of Philip II of Spain (1527-1598)*

A *map showing the journey of Raposo Tavares and the explorations of the Bandeirantes into the heart of their own country*

Raposo Tavares

Through their explorations, the Bandeirantes wiped out the imaginary line that divided the Portuguese and the Spanish. They left São Paulo in Brazil and followed the rivers that flowed west. They traveled as far as they could in order to extend the boundaries of their country and search for gold. The most remarkable of these travelers was Raposo Tavares, whose expedition on foot took four years and covered 7,400 miles. Tavares traveled through what is now Paraguay and Bolivia, up the Madeira River to the Amazon, from the Atlantic Ocean to the Andes Mountains, and from the Tropic of Capricorn to the equator.

Gold Mines

Until the mid-eighteenth century the Bandeirantes roamed the interior in search of diamonds and gold and new cities were founded. The capital of Brazil changed from Bahia, near the sugar plantations, to Rio de Janeiro, near the mines. Most of the wealth from these areas was sent to Portugal and then to England, which supplied Portugal and Brazil with manufactured (factory-made) goods. Part of this wealth paid for more and more African slaves to work in the mines. Part of the money was used by the Roman Catholic church to build wonderful churches filled with gold, paintings, and sculptures. The Portuguese took gold and diamonds from Latin America and did not build the economy up in return. For example, they abandoned road building and made weaving a crime. Their aim was to prevent goods produced in Latin America competing with goods shipped into the continent from Portugal.

The *Catholic church built many churches, and Catholicism is the main religion of modern-day Latin America.*

Coming of Age

Time for Change

Latin America produced gold, silver, emeralds, and diamonds, which ships carried to Europe along with wood, sugar, tobacco, and cotton. Spain and Portugal had a **monopoly** on all trade, and they imposed heavy taxes on their colonies.

The criollos were people with European parents who were born in Latin America. The criollos wanted a bigger share of government and more power, but the slaves and original inhabitants of Latin America did most of the work and owned very little. Gradually people began to demand freedom from colonization.

Meanwhile, in Britain, the **Industrial Revolution** (second half of the eighteenth century) was beginning. This commercial revolution required raw materials to make new products and people to buy the products in order to succeed. But the slaves and poor people of Latin America had no wealth and could not buy anything. International pressure against slavery was growing stronger and stronger.

Pineapples and maize came to Europe via Latin America.

34

African slaves washing gold in the Brazilian highlands. This engraving is by Johann Moritz Rugendas (1802-1858).

An engraving of Toussaint L'Ouverture in European military dress

The Europeans didn't come only in search of gold and slaves—they also came for trade. Latin America gave Europe valuable dyes and new foods such as maize, potatoes, tomatoes, and peanuts.

Rebel Republics

At the beginning of the seventeenth century, African slaves began to escape from the plantations in the northeast of Brazil. They explored inland and founded Palmares, a republic in the middle of a forest. Soon, slaves were escaping from every plantation to go there. They fought a fierce **guerrilla war** against the Portuguese, and their republic survived for over a century.

In the Caribbean, in 1791, a former slave from the French colony of St. Domingue, named Toussaint L'Ouverture (1746-1803), led a rebellion. In only eight years L'Ouverture managed to abolish slavery, defeat the French army, and establish the independent Republic of Haiti.

Fighting for Freedom

Brazil made several attempts to gain independence during the eighteenth century. The most significant one was led by Joaquim José de Silva Xavier (1748-1792), known as Tiradentes, in 1789. However, many wealthy Brazilians were more interested in keeping slavery. When the country finally became independent in 1822, it did so as a kingdom under the rule of a Portuguese prince. The end of slavery did not come until 1888 and the monarchy survived until 1889, when the republic was established.

Spanish America was divided into provinces and **viceroyalties** by the eighteenth century. The struggle for independence was unsuccessful for a long time. Property owners became involved in the fight for freedom after the collapse of the Spanish monarchy, when Napoleon Bonaparte (1769-1821) invaded Spain in 1808.

The year 1810 was very important for freedom in Latin America. In Venezuela, Francisco de Miranda (1750-1816) led a war of independence over a period of two years, but was eventually betrayed and imprisoned by the Spaniards. But the battle for Venezuela was eventually won by Simón Bolívar in 1821.

In 1811, in Mexico, a priest named Miguel Hidalgo y Castilla (1753-1811) led an armed rebellion against the Spanish. He was defeated and killed but was immediately replaced by another priest, José María Morelos y Pavón (1765-1815), who tried to abolish slavery and establish a republic. Morelos was shot in 1815 and Mexico did not become independent until 1821, when it was ruled by an army officer, and then became a republic in 1824.

Simón Bolívar

Simón Bolívar (1783-1830) was known as "the Liberator." Bolívar freed his home of Venezuela in 1821, Colombia and Ecuador in 1822, Peru in 1824, and Bolivia (named after him) in 1825. Bolívar started fighting the Spanish in Venezuela in 1810 but was defeated and had to flee the country. Bolívar was president of Gran Colombia (a union of Venezuela, Colombia, and Ecuador) from 1822 to 1830.

A *French engraving of Mexico City showing the cathedral and main square, from* Voyage Pittoresque en Mexique (Picturesque Voyage Through Mexico) *of 1836, by Carl Nebel*

A *map showing some of the major battles San Martín and Bolívar fought to bring independence to Latin America*

T*his detail of the Mexican* Independence Mural *(1960) by Juan O'Gorman shows Father Hidalgo in the center holding up a flaming torch and Simón Bolívar standing to his right.*

A Unified Nation

After securing the independence of Venezuela, Simón Bolívar went on a campaign to free Colombia and Ecuador. His dream was to unify all the Spanish-speaking countries in one free, rich, and powerful state.

During the same period, another general, José de San Martín (1778-1850), came from Spain in 1812 to join a rebellion in Buenos Aires in Argentina, which later led to the independence of Argentina and Paraguay. San Martín crossed the Andes Mountains with the Chilean Bernardo O'Higgins, at the head of a well-prepared army, and freed Chile in 1817-1818. With ships under the command of Lord Cochrane (a Scottish adventurer), he landed his troops on the Peruvian coast in 1820 and forced the Spaniards to take refuge in the mountains. Two years later, San Martín and Bolívar met and decided that the final attack against Spanish power in America would be made by Bolívar. The Battle of Ayacucho was won by Bolívar's general Antonio José de Sucre (1795-1830), in 1824. Sucre went on to become the first president of Bolivia, in 1826.

In less than 15 years of war, most of Latin America was free—except for Cuba and Puerto Rico, which remained colonies until 1898. But Bolívar's dream of a united Latin America did not come true because the differences among regions were too great.

6 Visitors and Travelers

Travelers' Tales

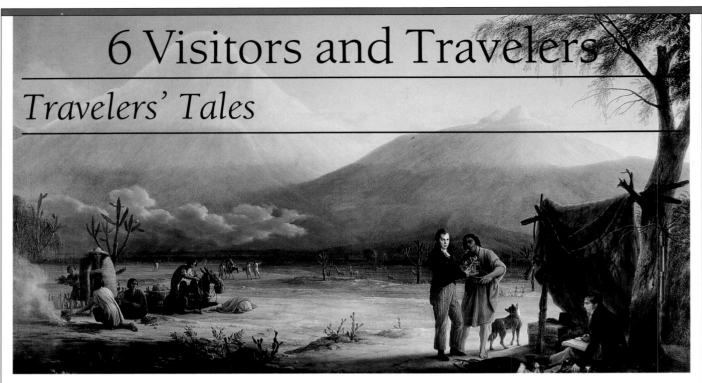

Eighteenth-century Scientists Explore

During the eighteenth century, geographical and scientific societies sponsored expeditions all over Latin America. In 1735 the French Academy of Sciences sent 11 scientists to take measurements under the line of the equator. These investigators eventually proved correct Sir Isaac Newton's theory that the earth is larger at the equator. Their calculation of the length of the equator was the basis for all measurements of length, volume, and weight in the metric system.

La Condamine and Ferreira

The leader of the French Academy expedition was Charles-Marie de la Condamine (1701-1774). La Condamine was a mathematician who was also interested in natural history, astronomy, and cartography. La Condamine explored over 2,400 miles of the Amazon region, examining plants, birds, animals, people, and the landscape as he went. On his return to Paris in 1745, La Condamine published accounts of his journeys across the "new" continent and inspired interest in the exploration of Latin America among scientists, **botanists**, cartographers, and artists all over Europe.

It wasn't just European scientists who were investigating Latin America. Alexandre Rodrigues Ferreira (1756-1815) was born in Brazil and trained as a natural historian in Portugal. Ferreira returned to Brazil in 1783 to explore the rivers of his homeland and write papers on tribes and their masks, pipes, pottery, and huts.

A *painting of Humboldt (center, right) and Bonpland (bottom right-hand corner) with the mountain of Chimborazo in the background*

Alexander von Humboldt

The most important scientist to explore Latin America during the colonial period was a German, Alexander von Humboldt (1769-1859). Humboldt spent five years with the French botanist Aimé Bonpland (1773-1858) studying Central America and the Andes. Humboldt wrote 30 books about the highlands, volcanoes, rain forests, geography, politics, and economy of Latin America.

A *drawing of a black-headed Cacajao monkey, from one of Humboldt and Bonpland's books on the animals of Latin America*

Nineteenth-century Scientists Explore

Carl Friedrich Philip von Martius (1794-1868) traveled to Brazil in 1818 to investigate tribal Indians and natural history. Martius returned to Europe two years later with a collection of plant specimens and Indian artifacts. The studies Martius made were important in establishing academic writing on Brazilian Indians after this time. His collection of 6,500 plants formed the basis of the *Flora Braziliensis*, which was a catalog of Latin American plants written with the zoologist Johann Baptist von Spix (1781-1826).

The Frenchman Alcide Orbigny (1802-1857) sailed for Rio de Janeiro. Orbigny explored Argentina, Paraguay, Cuba, Venezuela, Colombia, and Bolivia. In 1829 he explored Patagonia for nine months, eventually visiting the Tehuelche Indians and going on an ostrich hunt.

The Englishmen Henry Walter Bates (1825-1892) and Alfred Russel Wallace (1823-1913) traveled to the Amazon in 1848 to collect anything they could find to further their knowledge of Latin America. Wallace lost his precious specimens and notes at sea, but when Bates returned to England in 1859 he took with him huge collections that included over 3,000 newly discovered species of insect.

The German Karl von den Steinen (1855-1929) was one of the last great explorer-scientists of the nineteenth century. Steinen's two-volume work on the remote Indians of Brazil was of major scientific importance.

An engraving of explorers making their way through the rain forest, from Carl Nebel's Voyage Pittoresque en Mexique *(Picturesque Voyage Through Mexico) of 1836*

A *painting by Debret*

Piecing Together the Puzzle

Most scientific expeditions published accounts of their journeys relating new discoveries and providing maps. Little by little, European knowledge of rivers, mountains, and the entire continent of Latin America became more accurate— it was as if the map of the continent was a jigsaw puzzle and each expedition supplied a new piece of the picture.

Naturalists drew new plants and animals, and artists made sketches of entire areas. The Frenchman Jean-Baptiste Debret (1768-1848) spent 15 years in Brazil painting everything he saw in great detail. On his return to France in 1831, Debret published three volumes of pictures of Latin American life. The German artist Johann Moritz Rugendas drew ordinary scenes in Brazil, Mexico, Chile, Peru, and Bolivia.

The Race for Knowledge

Colonel Fawcett disappeared while exploring in search of legendary ancient Indian cities deep in the rain forests of Brazil.

Charles Lindbergh (1902-1974) flew over the Atlantic Ocean in 1927. He later explored Latin America from the air (bottom right), in search of the ruins of lost civilizations.

Lost and Found Cities

In 1909, the Englishman Colonel Percy Fawcett (1867-1925) was hired by the Bolivian government to study a river on the border with Brazil. After this expedition to the Brazilian highlands, Fawcett saw an eighteenth-century document mentioning a fabulous "lost city," complete with silver mines. In 1920 Fawcett organized an unsuccessful expedition to look for the city. He returned to Brazil in 1925 and explored with his son and a friend, but they all disappeared without trace in the Amazon region.

Other important cities were rediscovered. In Peru, the American archaeologist Dr. Hiram Bingham (1875-1919) found the ruins of Machu Picchu near Cuzco (see

An explorer's boat being hauled up a waterfall in 1876.

pages 22-23) in 1911. In Central America important Maya ruins were spotted from an airplane (see page 15). More recently, the ruins of the Aztec temple destroyed by Cortés were found in the main square of Mexico City (see page 36) when workmen were digging a new subway in the 1980s.

La Condamine's Journey 1735
Humboldt and Bonpland's Journey 1800-1803
Bates's Journey 1849-59
Bates and Wallace's Journey 1848
Wallace's Journey 1848-52
Orbigny's Journey 1830
Martius's Journey 1818-20
Fawcett's Journey 1925

All Types of Explorers

The former American president Theodore Roosevelt (1858-1919) made a scientific expedition to Brazil and wrote a book about his journey. The French **anthropologist** Claude Lévi-Strauss (1908-1990) lived among the Brazilian Indians in order to study their culture. The British botanist and artist Margaret Mee (1909-1988) made many journeys to the Amazon region to study the unusual plants, and the French **oceanographer** Jacques Cousteau (b.1910) specially adapted his ship *Calypso* to explore the Amazonian environment.

Theodore Roosevelt with the first jaguar he shot on his expedition to the Rio da Dúvida (renamed Roosevelt) in 1913-1914

7 Modern Times

Wealth and Poverty

Modern Latin America is made up of 22 independent (no longer colonized) countries. But home government did not instantly bring economic wealth. Former Spanish and Portuguese colonies were still under a great deal of foreign influence long after independence.

Producing Food to Export

The newly independent nations of Latin America were free to trade with countries other than Spain and Portugal. At the time when Europe was dominated by the Industrial Revolution (see page 34) new manufactured goods were sent all around the globe, thanks to railroads and steamships. The new European products needed large supplies of raw materials, and Latin America specialized in supplying some of these materials. The economic growth that followed was based on the production of goods such as copper, sugar, rubber, and cotton for international markets. Agricultural land was planted with crops grown for export rather than those needed for the local people. New local industries were not protected and many collapsed when faced with competition from large and powerful foreign companies.

A newly built railroad bridge crosses a valley in the Andes Mountains (Peru) in the 1870s.

The Panama Canal was built from 1904 to 1914 across Central America. This photograph was taken the day the canal opened.

Railroads and Steamships

New technology brought many changes to Latin America. Steamships made mass transportation of goods possible and remote regions were more fully explored. There was no complete network of railroads. Most of the railroad lines had been built to transport goods for export. Some connected the mines to the ports and others were built where river navigation was difficult. When mass production of cars began in North America (1908), it became possible to travel through the continent more easily.

These Amazon Indians (c.1900) were forced to work in the rubber forests.

A Few Rich People

The wealth produced by this sudden development was unevenly distributed. The landowners became rich, bought more land, and got richer. The ordinary people had to survive on very low wages and could not afford to own land. The workers couldn't move away to find something better because they were always in debt to the employer's shop, which was usually the only one in the area.

The prices of the raw materials Latin America sold dropped lower and lower, while the prices of goods produced by Europe got higher and higher. The countries outside Latin America were still richer and still controlled the Latin American economy to a certain extent.

The International Debt

International banks opened branches in Latin America to safeguard their investments in cattle, **nitrates**, copper, rubber, sugar, coffee, cotton, and other products. Money was lent to Latin American governments by foreign governments for investment in railroads, ports, roads, water and sewage systems, gas, electric power and, later, telephones. Most public services (like railroads) were owned by foreign companies. The massive interest payments on these initial loans are still being paid off by Latin America today.

Cândido Rondon (1865-1958)

The Brazilian Cândido Rondon served in the army throughout his long life. When he died he was known as "the Marshall of Peace." He traveled through the wilderness for 40 years, mostly on foot, on horseback, and in canoes, covering nearly 25,000 miles, which is the circumference of the earth itself. Rondon erected telegraph lines through the jungle, inspected frontiers, explored unknown territory throughout Brazil, and made contact with many isolated Indian tribes. Even when attacked, his troops always followed his command to "Die, if necessary. But never kill." Rondon ran the Indian Protection Service from 1910 until his death in 1958. Through this agency he championed the rights of native Latin American Indians.

A young boy earns his living as a street trader in Lima, Peru.

Despite the transportation revolution of the last 100 years, traditional types of travel are still essential, such as this donkey used to collect crops in southern Brazil.

Latin America Today

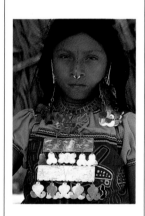

The mixture of rich and poor housing in the city of Rio de Janeiro, Brazil

Traditional cultures have survived even in areas known to Europeans for 500 years – a native from Brazil.

A Kayapó Indian uses a video camera to inform people about his culture.

Exploring Through Building

The opening of the Panama Canal in 1914 linked the Pacific and the Atlantic Oceans and made it even easier to travel or transport goods across the world. Building railroads, roads, and waterways often meant traveling through unexplored territory in difficult conditions.

Moving to the Cities

With new ways of traveling across the continent, poor people left the countryside and went to the cities in search of work. Many of these people found jobs in new factories and plantations. Slums grew up in cities because of the increasing population. Today, some Latin American cities, such as Mexico City and São Paulo, are among the largest in the world.

Immigration and Emigration

In the last century Latin America has welcomed immigrants from Europe and Asia. Europeans in particular were attracted by favorable immigration laws. They wanted to explore a different continent where there was plenty of land, the population was scarce, and new labor was needed because of the end of slavery and the success of new industries. Many more Europeans emigrated to Latin America between 1880 and 1914 than in the previous three and a half centuries. Apart from the Portuguese and Spanish, who have lived in Latin America since colonial times, Italians, Germans, Poles, Swiss, French, Ukrainians, Lebanese, Japanese (mainly in Brazil), and Chinese (in Peru, Cuba, Mexico, and Panama) have all come to settle since the turn of the century.

NORTH AMERICA

MEXICO

Gulf of Mexico

• Mexico City

CENTRAL
AMERICA

• Havana   Guantanamo
CUBA   DOMINICAN
              REPUBLIC
Port au Prince Santo   San Juan
• Belize   Domingo
BELIZE   HAITI   PUERTO
GUATEMALA • Guatemala   RICO
HONDURAS
EL SALVADOR • Tegucigalpa
San Salvador • Managua   CARIBBEAN SEA
NICARAGUA

COSTA RICA • San José   • Caracas
        Panama
PANAMA   VENEZUELA   GUYANA
                                      FRENCH
        COLOMBIA   SURINAM GUIANA

        • Bogotá

                              Amazon River

Galapagos Islands
        • Quito
        ECUADOR   • AMAZON BASIN

                    SOUTH AMERICA

        PERU   BRAZIL

        • Lima

                    BOLIVIA
                                  • Brasilia
                    • La Paz

PACIFIC
OCEAN   PARAGUAY   • Rio de Janeiro
                                  Asunción   São Paulo •
        CHILE
                    ARGENTINA

The countries of
modern-day Latin
America and their
capital cities

                              URUGUAY
        • Santiago   Buenos Aires • • Montevideo

Still Exploring Today

Being tolerant is said to be a very distinctive part of
Latin American culture. The people of Latin America
have lived through tough economic times and political
instability that has led to a series of revolutions,
military coups, civil wars, and general social
unrest. These events have been, and continue
to be, a result of Latin America's violent
history, but the rich mixture of people
living in, visiting, and exploring the
continent is something of which
Latin Americans are very proud.

Soccer is the most
popular sport in Latin
America. This is the
national stadium in
Lima, Peru.

Cape Horn

Latin America	Europe	Other
c.6600 B.C. Evidence of maize and squash being farmed in Ecuador.	**c.6500 B.C.** Farming begins in Greece and spreads to other areas of Europe.	**c.5000 B.C.** Farming begins in western parts of India.
c.5000 Farming begins in Mexico. **c.2000** Farming throughout Latin America.	**c.3000** Use of copper spreads throughout Europe.	**c.2500** The horse is domesticated in Central Asia.
c.1200-400 The Olmec culture (Mexico). **c.1200-300** The Chorrera culture (Andes).	**c.1600** Mycenaean civilization begins in Greece.	**c.1500** The use of iron begins in Turkey. **c.1200** The Jewish religion emerges.
c.850-200 The Chavín culture (Peru). **c.600-200** The Paracas culture (Peru).	**510** The Roman Republic is founded.	**c.650** Iron is being used in China. **c.230** The Great Wall of China is built.
c.1-600 A.D. The city of Teotihuacán is built.	**43 A.D.** The Roman Empire invades Britain.	**30 A.D.** Death of Jesus Christ. Spread of Christianity begins.
c.1-700 A.D. The Moche culture (Andes).	**117** The Roman Empire is at its greatest extent.	**300s** The Ghanian Empire is founded in West Africa
c.300-900 The Mayan civilization is powerful.	**c.542** Bubonic plague spreads through Europe.	**622** Muhammad founds the religion of Islam in Arabia.
900-1200 The Toltec and Chichimec peoples.	**959** The Unification of England.	**935** The text of the Koran finished. **960** Song Dynasty in China.
c.1100-1530 The Incas found the city of Cuzco and build their empire.	**1066** The Normans conquer England.	**c.1000** The Vikings colonize Greenland and travel to America.
c.1345-1530 The Aztec civilization.	**1340s** The Bubonic plague continues to spread throughout Europe.	**1352** Ibn Battuta travels to Africa. **1368** Ming Dynasty in China.
1492 Christopher Columbus arrives in Latin America. **1494** The Treaty of Tordesillas is signed.	**1492** The first globe is made in Germany by Martin Behaim.	**1498** The Portuguese (led by Vasco da Gama) arrive in India.
1519 Magellan sails around the world. **1519-21** The conquest of Mexico by Cortés. **1532-33** The conquest of Peru by Pizarro.	**1532** John Calvin starts the Protestant movement in France.	**1530s** The European slave trade begins across the Atlantic Ocean.
1550-1690s Jesuit missionaries explore the interior in search of converts.	**1618** The Thirty Years War of religion starts.	**1607** The first English settlement is founded in America (Virginia).
c.1660-1750s The Bandeirantes explore Brazil.	**1667** The French begin to expand under Louis XIV.	**1644** Manchu Dynasty in China. **1680** Rozvi Empire in Zimbabwe.
1791-99 Toussaint L'Ouverture leads a rebellion of black slaves.	**1756** The Seven Years War begins. **1789** The French Revolution begins.	**c.1700s** European exploration of Africa. **1775-83** The American Revolution.
1810-12 Francisco de Miranda leads an unsuccessful war of independence in Venezuela.	**1807** The slave trade is abolished in Britain.	**1789** George Washington becomes the first president of the United States.
1817-18 San Martín liberates Chile. **1821-22** Mexico, Venezuela, Colombia, Ecuador, and Brazil become independent.	**1884-85** The West African conference is held in Berlin (Germany).	**1857** The Indian mutiny. **1861** The American Civil War begins.
1898 Cuba and Puerto Rico become independent. **1904-14** Building of the Panama Canal.	**1914-18** World War I.	**c.1915** Africa continues to be divided by foreign powers. **1917** The U.S. enters World War I.
1932-35 Paraguay and Bolivia fight over the Chaco region.	**1939-45** World War II.	**1941** The U.S. enters World War II.
1962 The Cuban missile crisis takes place between President Kennedy and Soviet leader Khrushchev.	**1961** The Berlin Wall is built in Germany.	**1961** John F. Kennedy becomes president of the United States. **1963** John F. Kennedy is assassinated.
1970s Many Latin American countries are ruled by military dictatorships.	**1972** The European Community gains more members.	**1965-73** The United States is involved in the Vietnam War.
1980s Peru, Argentina, Brazil, and Chile hold democratic elections.	**1985** Mikhail Gorbachev becomes the leader of the Soviet Union.	**1981** Ronald Reagan becomes president of the United States.
1992 Brazil hosts the United Nations Conference on the Environment and Development (the Earth Summit).	**1989** The Berlin Wall falls. **1990** Boris Yeltsin becomes leader of Russia. East and West Germany are united.	**1989** Pro-democracy demonstrators are killed in Tiananmen Square, Beijing, China. **1993** Bill Clinton becomes the president of the United States.

Glossary

A

alpaca: an animal (about three feet tall) that is related to the camel family and looks like a goat. The alpaca is valued for its hairy coat, which can be made into very fine wool.

anthropologist: someone who studies human beings and their cultures.

aqueduct: a human-made channel for water.

archaeologist: someone who studies the past by searching for and examining objects from early societies.

artifact: an ancient object.

B

botanist: someone who studies plants.

C

caravans: a group of merchants traveling across land to sell their goods (usually carried by horses, camels, or donkeys).

civil war: war between people of the same country.

colonize: to settle in another land while still keeping ties with the original country. Sometimes the settlers take over the new land by force and claim it.

E

estuary: the place where a river joins the sea. Estuaries contain a mixture of both fresh and salt water and have tides.

equation: a mathematical formula.

equator: an imaginary line which circles the earth at an equal distance from both the North and South Poles.

evaporate: to change a liquid into a gas by using heat or moving air.

F

fertile: describes soil in which plants grow easily; it is moist and full of minerals for the plants to feed on.

fluvial basin: land carved into the shape of a large basin by the movement of a river.

G

geological: relating to the science of geology. Geology is the study of the structure and history of the earth.

guerrilla war: a war fought by soldiers who do not belong to an official, national army. Guerrillas use different fighting tactics from official armies, usually involving ambushes and sabotage.

I

Industrial Revolution: a period of social and economic change beginning in Britain in the 1760s. It involved the change from people producing goods at home to working in large factories with newly invented machines.

irrigation: the watering of land and crops with a system of **aqueducts**.

J

Jesuit: a member of the Roman Catholic Order of Jesus, founded by St. Ignatius in the sixteenth century. The Jesuits traveled all over the world working as missionaries.

M

manioc: a plant **native** to Latin America that is grown for its roots. The roots are ground down and used to make bread and tapioca.

military coup: when the army of a country takes over its government by force.

monopoly: domination by one particular country or company of a service, or product. When this situation occurs, the company who holds the monopoly can dictate the price of the product or service.

N

native: a person, plant, or animal that belongs to a certain place.

nitrates: chemicals used in explosives and fertilizers.

O

oceanographer: someone who studies the plants, animals, and environments of the world's oceans.

P

pampas: the flat area of land in Argentina between the Andes Mountains and the Atlantic Ocean.

passage: a trading route of the fifteenth and sixteenth centuries.

pilgrimage: a journey made by a follower of a religion to a place of special religious significance.

Q

Quimbaya: a community of Indians who lived in the central mountain range of Colombia. The Quimbaya made large and intricate objects out of gold such as helmets, masks, and crocodile pendants.

R

republic: an independent country which has no monarch and is ruled by an elected government.

S

Sinu: a culture that existed during the fourteenth century in what is now Colombia. They lived by gathering food and fishing in the Magdalena River valleys. The Sinu were very skilled in the art of casting and hammering gold ornaments.

T

Tairona: the dominant civilization of northeastern Colombia from 1000 A.D. up to the fourteenth and fifteenth centuries. The Tairona were the finest goldsmiths of the area and built stone houses and roads.

textile: any material woven from spun threads, such as wool and cotton.

Tolima: a people who lived in the middle of the Magdalena Valley in northern Colombia. They were excellent goldsmiths.

tropical: the climate of the earth between the Tropic of Cancer and the Tropic of Capricorn. These are two imaginary lines the same distance north and south of the **equator**. The tropical areas of the world are usually very hot and the land is very **fertile**.

Turks: people from Turkey (in southern Europe, next to Greece).

V

viceroyalties: places governed by viceroys, people appointed by a monarch to rule a colony.

Y

yam: a **tropical** plant, the root of which is eaten like a vegetable.

Index

Numbers in **bold** indicate an illustration. Words in **bold** are in the glossary on page 47.